Once a Wolf

How Wildlife Biologists Fought to Bring Back the Gray Wolf

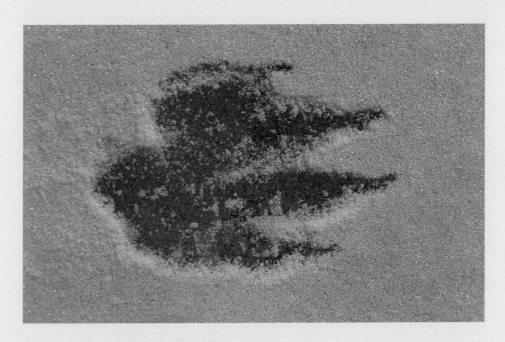

Stephen R. Swinburne

with photographs by Jim Brandenburg

HOUGHTON MIFFLIN COMPANY ■ BOSTON

To my in-laws, Rodger and Joyce Wolf, who raised a great Wolf pack —S. R. S.

Text copyright © 1999 by Stephen R. Swinburne
Photographs copyright © 1999 by Jim Brandenburg

www.hmhbooks.com

Library of Congress Cataloging-in-Publication Data

Swinburne, Stephen R.
    Once a wolf : how wildlife biologists fought to bring back the gray wolf / Stephen R. Swinburne ;
with photographs by Jim Brandenburg.
    p. cm.
    Includes bibliographical references and index.
    Summary: Surveys the history of the troubled relationship between wolves and humans, examines the
view that these predators are a valuable part of the ecosystem, and describes the conservation movement
to restore them to the wild.
    RNF ISBN 0-395-89827-7 PAP ISBN 0-618-11120-4
    [1. Wolves — West (U.S) — Juvenile literature. 2. Wildlife reintroduction —Yellowstone National
Park — Juvenile literature. [1. Wolves. 2. Endangered species. 3. Wildlife reintroduction.]
    I. Brandenburg, Jim, ill. II. Title.
    QL737.C22S836 1999
    333.95'977316'0978752 — DC21

                                               98-16865
                                             CIP
                                             AC

Book design by Chris Hammill Paul
Printed in China

SCP 20 19 18
4500426496

Contents

Then God spoke to the wolf, saying, "From this time on you are accused.
You shall hide from the light of day and hunt by night, and the hand of
every man shall be against you." And so it was.

    —Marchen und Sagen der Sudslaven, *1883, from* The Heavenly Zoo:
    Legends and Tales of the Stars, *retold by Alison Lurie, 1979.*

Milo Winter, from "The Wolf and The Shepherd," from *The Aesop for Children*, 1919

In "The Wolf and the Shepherd," one of Aesop's fables, a shepherd is lulled into believing he can leave his flock of sheep in the care of a wolf while he goes on an errand. But as Aesop tells us, "When he came back and saw how many of the flock had been killed and carried off, the shepherd knew how foolish it was to trust a wolf. Once a wolf, always a wolf."

One ■

"Beast of Waste and Desolation"

HATRED OF WOLVES goes far back in history. As soon as people began raising livestock, wolves became the enemy and the symbol of savagery. In 5000 B.C., the earliest farmers of Asia killed wolves to protect cattle, sheep, and other domestic animals. Aesop, a slave living in Greece around 600 B.C., wrote many stories that painted the wolf as a cunning and greedy beast. References to the wolf in the Bible depict the animal as villainous and sly. In the New

Gustave Doré, "Little Red Riding Hood," from *Perrault's Fairy Tales,* 1867

Children learn to fear wolves at an early age.

Testament, in Matthew 7:15, it is written, "Beware of false prophets, which come to you in sheep's clothing, but inwardly they are ravening wolves."

The wolf's bad reputation spread throughout Europe. In fairy tales and legends, wolves were evil. Who has not read "The Three Little Pigs" and "Little Red Riding Hood"? The myth of the wicked wolf became part of our culture.

People learned to fear wolves because they killed livestock. But the more ancient terror of wolves attacking humans turned fear to hatred. From Russia and France to China and the Middle East came bloody stories of wolves killing and eating people. Our innate fear of large predators becomes distorted after reading stories and poems such as Robert Browning's "Ivan Ivanovitch." The poem, which takes place in Russia, tells of a wolf pack chasing a horse-drawn sleigh full of people through the winter woods. To save their lives, the adults throw their children to the wolves.

England hated wolves from the country's beginning. King Edward, who ruled in the tenth century, allowed citizens to pay their taxes in wolf heads. Around 1500, entire forests were burned to destroy wolves. To protect livestock, laws aimed at exterminating these creatures were passed. The last wolf in Scotland was killed around 1743. All of Ireland's wolves were destroyed by 1776.

The Europeans who settled America in the seventeenth century brought their hatred of wolves to this continent. There were plenty of wolves to hate. Some estimate that 250,000 wolves flourished in the vast forests of the New World. Other than humans, the wolf was once the most widely distributed mammal in the Northern Hemisphere.

The general feeling about wildlife in colonial times is summed up in the Reverend Cotton Mather's words: "What is not useful is vicious." Colonists feared the forest,

In North America, there is no record of a healthy wild wolf killing or seriously injuring a person. In fact, wolves are shy creatures and avoid people if at all possible.

Wolves are carnivores, feeding on deer, caribou, elk, and moose as well as birds and small mammals. Scientists believe that wolves can go two weeks or longer without food. They eat when they get the chance, often gorging on twenty pounds of meat at a time. This pattern of feasting and fasting helps them survive.

calling it "a waste and howling wilderness." They chopped down trees to carve out fields and pastures for their cattle, pigs, horses, and sheep. They also killed many deer and other native prey of the wolf. When their usual prey were decimated, wolves attacked domestic animals to keep themselves alive. The wolf was seen as an obstacle to civilization and progress, and thus began the battle between man and wolf on American soil.

"It is ordered, that every English man that killeth a wolf in any part within the limits of this patent shall have allowed him 1d [one penny]." A penny per wolf was the first bounty established by the Massachusetts Bay Company in 1630. By 1640 the price had risen to 40 shillings per wolf, or $4.80, then an average month's salary. Many settlers, tempted by the good pay, hunted wolves. Even Native Americans, who traditionally revered the wolf, were encouraged to kill them. A Massachusetts law of 1644 stated that an Indian who brought in a dead wolf was to be rewarded with either three quarts of wine or a bushel of corn. Res-

Wolves lead wild, secret lives. They find all they need — food, home, territory — in wilderness. Left alone, wolves thrive.

idents of Cape Cod were so fearful of wolves that in 1717 they considered putting up a fence to keep them out.

By the early 1800s New England farmers had beaten the wolf. Through hunting, encouraged by state bounties, and through killing off deer and altering habitat, they had wiped out their enemy. The last wolf in New England was destroyed in Maine in 1860.

If the fight against the wolf in the East was a battle, the campaign in the West was all-out war. The building of railroads in the 1860s and 1870s led to the wholesale slaughter of wolves. As settlers and hunters cleared the land of native bison, great herds of Hereford and Angus cattle were set loose to graze on the western range. Ranchers made huge investments in the cattle business. With access to railroads, cattlemen shipped beef to eastern markets and reaped big profits. They weren't about to let anything harm their cattle, especially a predator.

Wolves have to eat. When the bison disappeared, they turned their attention to livestock. On some ranches, wolves killed nearly half the year's calves. Cowmen, in return, attacked the predators with a vengeance, using leg-hold traps, bullets, and poison. A new profession arose as "wolfers" were hired by ranchers to rid the land of wolves.

One early Montana rancher described a wolfer's job: "A wolfer's outfit was a pack horse, a saddle horse, flour, beans, sugar, coffee, and salt; a blanket, a buffalo robe, the best rifle he could procure, a good revolver, plenty of ammunition, a hunting knife and a supply of strychnine. These supplies were purchased in the fall at one of the trading posts and at the first freeze the wolfers took to the plains and did not return until spring."

In *The Last of the Loners*, a collection of stories about the last western wolves, Stanley Young wrote, "There was a sort of unwritten law of the range that no cowman would knowingly pass by a carcass of any kind without inserting in it a goodly dose of strychnine, in the hope of killing one more wolf."

The wolfers' poison worked. From 1850 to the 1880s, the greatest massacre of wolves in human history occurred in the American West. Strychnine was not selective. Along with the wolves, thousands of coyotes, foxes, badgers, wolverines, mountain

Pictured is Coyote Smith, a Wyoming wolf hunter, with a freshly killed wolf. About a decade later, Theodore Roosevelt, before becoming president, called the wolf a "beast of waste and desolation."

Wyoming Division of Cultural Resources

Photo courtesy of the National Archives

Wolfers became experts at setting traps. Here a wolf has stepped into the steel jaws of a trap near Decker, Wyoming, 1921.

lions, bald eagles, and other animals perished. But wolves were the main target. One historian reported that thousands were destroyed in the Montana territory every year from 1870 to 1877.

Native Americans could not understand the white man's war on the wolf. The Lakota, Blackfeet, and Shoshone, among other tribes, considered the wolf their spiritual brother. They respected the animals' endurance and hunting ability, and warriors prayed to hunt like them. They draped themselves in wolf skins and paws, hoping they would acquire the wolf's hunting skills of stealth, courage, and stamina. Plains Indians wore wolf-skin disguises on raiding parties. Elite Comanche warriors were called wolves.

Plains Indians hunted bison wearing wolf skins. The American artist George Catlin painted this picture in 1832.

National Museum of American Art, Smithsonian Institution

A government predator control agent killed this mother and her eleven newborn pups in March 1916. The practice of "denning," destroying entire families of wolves at the den, was common.

The war on the wolf by white settlers raged on. Western ranchers continued to claim that thousands of cattle were killed every year by wolves. In 1884, Montana created its first wolf bounty—one dollar for every dead wolf. Bounties on wolves increased from fifty cents in 1875 to eight dollars in 1893. Over a period of thirty-five years, more than eighty thousand wolf carcasses were submitted for bounty payments in Montana. The government was pressured to provide free poison. Finally, in 1914, ranchers persuaded the United States Congress to provide funds to exterminate wolves on public lands.

The last wolves in the American West died hard. No place was safe, not even the nation's first national park, Yellowstone. The park was created in 1872, and from its very beginning, poisoned carcasses were set out to kill wolves. Nearly 140 wolves were killed by park rangers in Yellowstone from 1914 to 1926. In October 1926 two wolf pups

were trapped near a bison carcass. They were the last animals killed in the park's wolf control program.

Ranchers had won the war against the wolf. Only in the northern woods of Wisconsin, Minnesota, and Michigan could the howl of native gray wolves be heard. The vast lands of the American West fell silent. The country had lost its greatest predator.

Around 1930, some people began to understand the difference between the wolf of legend and the wolf of fact.

Two ▪
The Early Conservationists

I N THE EARLY 1930s a great irony occurred in the history of American wildlife. About the same time that the last wolves were being exterminated, scientists began to rethink the role of predators. Attitudes were changing. Biologists and researchers from universities and museums challenged the usual view of wolves and other predators as animals that must be destroyed. Calls came for their preservation.

Scientist Paul Errington advanced the idea that predators help eliminate weaker animals and thereby keep the prey species strong.

Iowa State University Library/University Archives

Sigurd Olson was the first scientist to study and document the wolf's family and social behavior.

Don Albrecht, Northland College, Sigurd Olson Environmental Institute

Paul Errington was the first biologist to research the relationship between predators and their prey. In 1929 he began studying gray foxes and bobwhite quail. From his later studies, focusing on mink and muskrats in Iowa, Errington concluded, "Mink predation upon muskrats tends to be almost restricted to those individuals of the muskrat population that may be properly referred to as pushovers."

The first serious research on wolves was done by a Minnesota naturalist named Sigurd Olson, who was a biology instructor at Ely Junior College in northeastern Minnesota. In 1920 he began field-work in Superior National Forest. For more than eighteen years, Olson snowshoed, hiked, and canoed the north woods. He shared his observations with trappers and loggers. He sorted wolf fact from wolf fiction. His knowledge grew of wolf packs, their ranges, and the animal's role in the habitat. In 1938 he published a report in *Scientific Monthly* titled "The Size and Organization of the Pack." Olson discovered that "the great majority of the [wolf] killings are of old, diseased or crippled animals. Such purely salvage killings are assuredly not detrimental to either deer or moose, for without the constant elimination of the unfit, the breeding stock would suffer."

This new view suggested that predators were a valuable part of the ecosystem. It was a radical departure from the view held by most people that wolves were useless and vicious creatures. As more people watched and studied these animals, they began learning fascinating things about wolf society.

Why do wolves howl? Biologists think they do so to communicate with and locate one another before and after the hunt, to defend their territory from other packs, and to strengthen the social bonds within the family.

In 1939 the National Park Service asked a young biologist named Adolph Murie to study wolves and the wild Dall sheep in rugged Mount McKinley National Park in Alaska. Park officials wanted to know more about the relationship between these animals. Were wolves killing too many sheep? Should the Park Service begin a wolf-control program so tourists could see more sheep, as well as moose and caribou? Murie spent three years in the field, watching wolves hunt and observing sheep take shelter along the steep cliffs. After spending thousands of hours in the field and walking more than 1,700 miles of rough terrain in one year alone, Murie concluded that wolves and sheep were locked in a delicate balance. He examined 829 sheep skulls collected around wolf dens and found that nearly 90 percent of them came from sheep that were either very young (less than two years) or old (more than eight years). A skull, in particular the horns and

Wolf biologist Adolph Murie summarized his long study of wolves in Alaska with these words: "The strongest impression remaining with me after watching the wolves . . . was their friendliness toward each other."

teeth, tells scientists a lot about the age and condition of an animal. "Such predation," Murie wrote, "would seem to benefit the species over a long period of time. It indicates a normal predator/prey relationship in Mount McKinley National Park."

Murie published his findings, *The Wolves of Mount McKinley*, in 1944. His research, considered the first scientific analysis of wolf predation, helped change the government's policy of wolf control. Murie was also the first professional photographer to document wolves in the wild. His work influenced generations of wildlife managers and scientists.

As the science of wolf research advanced with the studies of Olson, Murie, and other biologists, a scientist and author named Aldo Leopold was forging a new environmental philosophy. After graduating from the Yale School of Forestry with a master's degree in 1909, Leopold headed west to begin his career as a forest ranger. He spent his first years with the Forest Service in Arizona and New Mexico. Like most government employees at the time, he supported the predator control program and killed wolves, mountain lions, coyotes, and bears. Early in his career Leopold wrote, "New Mexico is leading the West in the campaign for eradication of predatory animals. It must keep on. The sportsmen and the stockmen demand the eradication of lions, wolves, coyotes and bobcats."

But Leopold knew many leading scientists of the day, including Errington and Murie, and their work helped change his thinking about predators. In 1944 Leopold wrote one of the most influential essays ever published on wolves, "Thinking Like a Mountain," which was part of his most famous book, *A Sand County Almanac*. The essay revealed what happened when he and his Forest Service companions massacred a wolf family, an experience that marked a turning point in his life:

In those days we had never heard of passing up a chance to kill a wolf. In a second we were pumping lead into the pack. . . .When our rifles were empty, the old wolf was down, and a pup was dragging a leg into impassable slide-rocks.

We reached the old wolf in time to watch a fierce green fire dying in her eyes. I realized then, and have known ever since, that there was something new to me in those eyes—something known only to her and to the mountain. I was young then, and full of trigger-itch; I thought that because fewer wolves meant more deer, that no wolves would mean hunters' paradise. But after seeing the green fire die, I sensed that neither wolf nor mountain agreed with such a view.

From the 1930s until his death in 1948, Leopold was at the forefront of a new conservation movement. He was an internationally respected scientist and considered the father of wildlife conservation. More than any other person, Leopold fanned the flames of change in attitudes about wolves and other predators. His elegant writings described the basic concept of ecology, that all aspects of nature are related and interdependent. Leopold advocated the value of wilderness and of wolves.

During the unusually cold winter of 1948–49, an ice bridge formed between the Canadian mainland and Isle Royale, an island in Lake Superior. A pair of wolves crossed the bridge and made themselves at home on the island, hunting moose. In 1958 Durward Allen of Purdue University, a prominent wildlife biologist, began a study of the wolves of Isle Royale. Allen

Aldo Leopold was the first biologist to call for the return of the wolf to Yellowstone National Park.

Rolf O. Peterson

The study of the wolves of Isle Royale, Michigan, began in June 1958 and continues today. It's the longest ongoing wolf research project in history.

chose a twenty-year-old graduate student, L. David Mech, to research the wolf—moose relationship.

"I just couldn't believe it," Mech said at the time. "I never thought I'd get, in my life, to some place where I'd see a wolf track. Suddenly, my horizons were greatly expanded. I would see wolf tracks in my lifetime, and I might even see wolves."

Mech studied the wolves and moose of Isle Royale for three years, earning his Ph.D. from Purdue in 1962. He was the first scientist to study wolves from the air. The countless hours he spent in rickety old planes flying tight circles above the island gave Mech almost constant air sickness. But it also rewarded him with a bird's-eye view of wolves chasing and killing moose. Over the years, Mech has seen more wolves hunting than any other person alive. He believes one of his most important discoveries is that wolves are not unfailing killers.

On Isle Royale, Mech watched wolves hunt moose seventy-seven times, but saw only six kills. "The prey are always ahead of the predators," he says. "Wolves have to try very hard for anything they get. And that is contrary to the views of a lot of the public . . . who feel wolves can go around and kill any time they want. If people understood the prey's advantages, there'd be even more sympathy for the predator as being a helpless link in that system."

Hundreds of hours of field observation have shown biologists that wolves make a kill only 2 to 3 percent of the time when they hunt. Usually their prey escapes. When they do make a kill, wolves cooperate to bring down animals much larger than themselves.

Moose are the most formidable prey of wolves. A well-placed kick from a moose can crack a wolf's rib cage or split its head open. Sometimes a large moose or bull elk will stand its ground rather than flee a pack of wolves. Scientists have learned that most prey animals that stand their ground are young, strong, and healthy. If a moose stands its ground, the pack is likely to give up.

David Mech

A research biologist for the National Biological Service, L. David Mech has studied wolves and worked on behalf of wolf conservation for more than forty years.

Ever since arriving on Isle Royale in June 1958, Dave Mech has dedicated his life to wolf research. After leaving Isle Royale, he went on to study wolves in Montana, Alaska, Italy, Russia, India, and, most recently, the Canadian Arctic. In 1970 he published *The Wolf,* considered the bible of wolf science. Known as "Dr. Wolf" or "Wolfman," Mech is one of the world's foremost authorities on these animals. He forces us to think differently about them. In the final paragraph of *The Wolf,* Mech writes, "If the wolf is to survive, the wolf haters must be outnumbered. They must be outshouted, outfinanced, and outvoted. Their narrow and biased attitude must be outweighed by an attitude based on an understanding of natural processes. Finally their hate must be outdone by a love for the whole of nature, for the unspoiled wilderness, and for the wolf as a beautiful, interesting, and integral part of both."

In 1973 the United States chose threatened and endangered wildlife over economic development when it passed the Endangered Species Act.

Three ■
The Battle to Bring the Gray Wolf Home

IN 1944 Aldo Leopold was far ahead of his time when he proposed that wolves be returned to their home in Yellowstone National Park. Even with the support of researchers like David Mech, not much would be done about Leopold's proposal for close to thirty years.

But the turbulent decades of the 1960s and 1970s saw sweeping environmental changes. The publication of Rachel Carson's *Silent Spring* in 1962 awakened many to the potential poisoning of the earth. In 1969 two powerful environmental groups were formed: Greenpeace and Friends of the Earth. President Richard Nixon banned the poisoning of predators in 1972, and in 1973 the U.S. Congress passed one of the most important environmental laws of the century: the Endangered Species Act. This law protected entire ecosystems on which endangered species depend. Among its many conservation initiatives, the act banned the sale and trade of products made from any endangered species, such as tortoiseshell from sea turtles. It guaranteed protection for wolves by imposing a $10,000 fine and a jail sentence on anyone killing a wolf.

One of the mandates of the Endangered Species Act was to restore endangered wildlife to their original habitats. In 1972 President Nixon's administration held the first official meeting to discuss returning wolves to Yellowstone. To many biologists, Yellowstone seemed like the ideal place to restore wolves — a 2.2 million-acre wilderness. Here was a complete ecosystem, with one notable exception — the wolf.

The 1972 meeting opened the door to the actual program of wolf recovery. Everyone agreed on the need to make sure that no wolves were then living in the park. During the late 1960s sightings of wolves had been periodically reported in Yellowstone, although none had been confirmed. The Park Service hired researcher John Weaver, and from 1975 to 1977 he turned Yellowstone Park inside out. He never found a wolf. His 1978 report concluded, "In the past fifty years, a viable population has not reestablished, and the wolf niche appears essentially vacant. Therefore, I recommend restoring this native predator by introducing wolves to Yellowstone."

Horatio Burns, a third-generation rancher, runs 1,800 cattle on his 20,000-acre spread in Big Timber, Montana. Yellowstone Park is sixty miles south of Burns's ranch — a two-day walk for a wolf. "The last thing I need is another predator," he says. "United States farmers and ranchers feel very proud that 5 percent of us feed the rest of the nation. I'm here to feed people. We raised enough beef from this ranch last year to satisfy 5,000 Americans. It's not in my genes to see a wolf eat a cow."

Stephen R. Swinburne

Scientist and wolf conservationist Renée Askins worked for fourteen years to bring wolves back to Yellowstone.

To carry out the mandate of the Endangered Species Act, the federal government formed the Northern Rocky Mountain Wolf Recovery Team. This team of biologists and professors tackled the issue of when and how to bring wolves back into the western United States. In 1982 they released their plan, which called for wolves to be returned to two places in the West, including Yellowstone, by 1987.

While biologists and bureaucrats were thinking through their plans for bringing wolves back, the western ranching community was fighting hard to keep wolves out. "The time of the wolf is over," one sheep rancher said. "The wolf is like the buffalo and the dinosaur; his time has come and gone."

Despite public support for returning wolves to Yellowstone, the powerful livestock industry and influential western politicians hampered plans for the program. To most ranchers, reintroducing wolves was like inviting a murderer home for dinner. And many ranchers swore they'd deal with wolves in their own way — "Shoot, shovel, and shut up!" Wolf recovery symbolized unwanted change and was seen as a tool for the government to gain more control over property rights. The issue of restoring wolves to Yellowstone generated a loud and emotional debate throughout the West.

In 1981 a young wildlife biologist named Renée Askins stepped into the fray. She had studied wolves in Michigan and Indiana. Her passion for them matched the intensity of the anti-wolf ranching crowd. Armed with a scientist's knowledge of the facts and a gift for public speaking and media relations, Askins mounted a dynamic campaign on behalf of the wolves. In 1986 she founded the Wolf Fund to help return wolves to Yellowstone.

In schools, church basements, and Grange halls throughout the West, Askins took her message out on the road and into the heart of the foe. "When I talk about the wolf issue," said Askins, "I talk about the importance of wildness in our lives. It's wildness that heals us. We need contact with it, regardless of whether we live in the city or in the Alaskan wilderness. Wolves offer that sense of wildness—the way wolves move, the way they play, their unpredictability, their living on the edge of their endurance, savage and surviving out there."

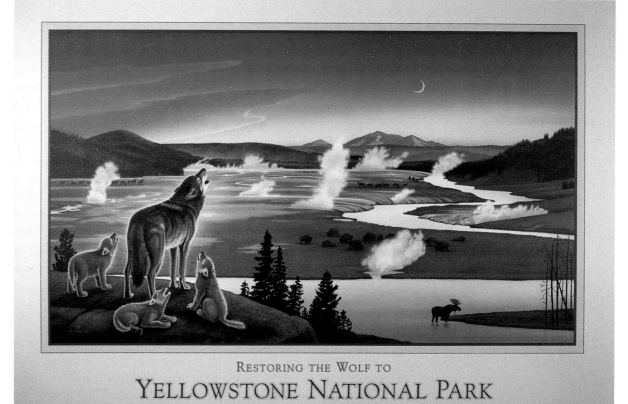

RESTORING THE WOLF TO
YELLOWSTONE NATIONAL PARK
DEFENDERS OF WILDLIFE

Monte Dolack Graphics

Ranchers felt that wolf recovery was being pushed down their throats by rich city people and easterners living far from any ranch. "They have the luxury of not worrying about livestock losses," the ranchers would claim.

"All the science, the studies, the experts, and the facts show that wolves kill far less than one percent of the livestock available to them," Askins often emphasized. "More cows and sheep die each year because of storms and dogs or because they've rolled over onto their backs and can't get up. The real issue is one of making room, and there is still a little room in the West—room for hunters, for environmentalists, for ranchers, and for wolves."

Defenders of Wildlife created this poster to help raise funds to compensate ranchers for livestock lost to wolves.

National Park Service

With no top predator to control their numbers, elk herds in Yellowstone National Park swelled to more than 30,000 animals by 1990. Biologists believe that predation by wolves helps control overpopulation of elk, moose, deer, and other grazing animals.

While Askins's Wolf Fund educated the public nationwide about the Yellowstone wolf issue, groups such as Defenders of Wildlife also played a key role. In 1985 Defenders sponsored an exhibit called "Wolves and Humans" at Yellowstone. More than 200,000 park visitors saw the exhibit. Defenders also established, a few years later, a simple and innovative plan: the wolf compensation fund. The idea was to pay ranchers for any live-stock killed by wolves. This went a long way to weaken the argument that livestock producers would bear the financial burden of the wolf reintroduction. Defenders' first payment was made in the summer of 1987, when a pack of Canadian wolves moved into

Montana and attacked and killed ten sheep and five cows. A month later Defenders sent checks totaling $3,000 to the ranchers who'd lost livestock.

In 1986 David Mech came out strongly in favor of restoring wolves. "The only thing missing in Yellowstone is the wolf," said Mech. "And the park can't really be wild without it. It's not complete or natural wilderness to have the species of prey that are there and not have the main predator they evolved with."

Finally, in 1991, Congress approved funding for an Environmental Impact Statement (EIS), which was required by law to be written before wolves could be returned to Yellowstone. The purpose of the EIS was to address every question or concern about wolves in Yellowstone, from the effects on the ecosystem to the cost of the program. The National Park Service budget for wolf recovery was estimated at $12 million. Ed Bangs, a wildlife biologist with the U.S. Fish and Wildlife Service, led the EIS team. Bangs knew returning wolves to Yellowstone was the toughest conservation issue in America's history. He also knew the issue would be decided politically. "Open houses" were held throughout the West to discuss wolf reintroduction. By the fall of 1993 Bangs had received 160,000 written comments, about 60,000 opposing the wolf's return and 100,000 in favor of it. He said it was the largest citizen response ever to a federal document.

Scientists have found bones and teeth of gray wolves in one of Yellowstone's caves. Wolves have been part of the ecosystem there for at least 1,300 years.

The Environmental Impact Statement was released in July 1994 and signed by Secretary of the Interior Bruce Babbitt. It called for the capture of wolves in Canada in November 1994 and their release in Yellowstone and central Idaho. Many conservationists believed that the final EIS came out in favor of wolf reintroduction because Congress had worked out a way to ease some provisions of the Endangered Species Act. Wolves in Yellowstone would be designated as an "experimental population" and ranchers would be allowed to shoot wolves found killing their livestock. This change in the rules helped break the deadlock between environmentalists and livestock producers.

The wolf had come almost full circle. From the centuries-long war against them to the early research by scientists such as Olson, Murie, and Leopold and finally to the twenty-five-year battle to bring them back, the wolves' destiny was once again to be shaped by humans. And yet this was a unique experiment. Would wolves adjust to a new environment? Would they turn north and walk back to their home in Canada? Would ranchers shoot them? No one knew.

Four ∎
Back on the Map

WHEN he was twelve years old, Doug Smith became enchanted with wilderness and wild animals. He remembers reading a *National Wildlife* article about the wolves of Minnesota. It changed his life. "There was something about the photographs—wolves bounding through snow and the way a wolf's eyes look right through you," says Smith. His passion for wolves grew as he learned more about them. At fifteen, he wrote to David Mech, asking for

volunteer work. It took some time to get an assignment, but he never gave up. During his last six weeks of high school, Smith worked on a real wolf project. Since grade school, Smith, now the leader of Yellowstone's wolf project, has devoted his life to studying wolves.

Smith and other wolf scientists used two methods, called hard release and soft release, to reintroduce wolves into the American West. Most reintroductions are hard releases. This method was used in Idaho, where wild wolves were released without first holding them in pens. A soft release, in which the wolves are kept in one-acre pens for up to ten weeks, was planned for Yellowstone. "We used this method because we wanted to reintroduce family groups into the park," said Smith. "We felt ten weeks in a pen together would maintain the group's strong social bonds so the animals would be less likely to split up once released. We also believed that holding them for that long would curb their natural desire to return home to Canada."

Doug Smith is currently the chief biologist with the Yellowstone wolf reintroduction project.

Biologists use a tried-and-true technique for catching wolves in the open and semiwooded habitats of Alberta, Canada. Skilled pilots fly fast, maneuverable helicopters just above the ground, and an expert aerial darter or "gunner," with a rifle loaded with a tranquilizer, takes an easy shot at a running wolf. Within minutes after a wolf is hit with a tranquilizer dart, it loses consciousness.

In December 1994 scientists captured twelve wild wolves in Canada. Eight were bound for Yellowstone, four for Idaho. Biologists knew they'd captured a special animal when they examined Number Nine. Seen up close, the black female wolf was beautiful. She lay blindfolded in a makeshift laboratory under mild anesthesia while veterinarians examined and measured her. She weighed ninety-eight pounds. They took a blood sample and analyzed it for rabies and other canine diseases. They checked for lice. They

National Park Service

This big black female wolf became known as Number Nine. She and her daughter, Number Seven, were captured in the rugged and wild country of Alberta, Canada.

Scientists can tell the age of a wolf by looking at its teeth. Pups lack wear on their molars and have pointed incisors and canines. Adult wolves' teeth become worn in the process of crunching bones and chewing meat. While plant eaters have flat molars, or back teeth, for mashing and chewing, wolves possess sharp front canines, or fangs, that can puncture the hide of an elk or clamp on to the rubbery nose of a moose. They are able to shear and tear meat and wolf down large chunks without chewing.

punched out a piece of flesh in each ear and inserted an identification number. The vets pulled back her dark lip and examined her teeth. The amount of wear told them she was four years old, prime breeding age. Blood seeping from her vagina indicated she was in heat, or estrus, and ready to mate. Because she was a mature female in heat, scientists believed that she was an alpha wolf, a leader of the pack. In a wolf pack's complex social structure, the dominant, or alpha, male and female are usually the only pair that breed and produce young.

On January 12, 1995, at 8:35 A.M., Number Nine entered Yellowstone National Park in an aluminum shipping container. With seven others of her kind, she had traveled by plane from Alberta, Canada, to Bozeman, Montana, a journey of over a thousand miles. Each wolf was fitted with a radio collar so that scientists could track and monitor its

School kids were given the day off to watch the wolves return to Yellowstone National Park.

Wolf biologists Mike Phillips, left, and Doug Smith prepare collars for the wolves so that scientists will be able to track the animals in the wild.

movements. Number Nine was transferred to a mule-drawn sled that carried her and her pup (Number Seven) to a remote enclosure in the park. Because wolves are good climbers, the chainlink pens were built in a circular fashion; the wolves might have climbed up a square corner and escaped. Armed guards patrolled the pens twenty-four hours a day.

On January 20, a magnificent silver-gray alpha male, Number Ten, newly arrived from Canada, was placed in the same pen with Number Nine and her pup. Doug Smith, together with Mike Phillips, another Yellowstone wolf biologist, hoped for a marriage between Nine and Ten, but they also feared a fight. No wolf in a pack has equal status with any other, and they will fight to determine dominance. Experience had shown that putting unrelated wolves together in captivity often leads to aggressive behavior, sometimes even death.

But no one told that to Number Ten and Number Nine. It wasn't long before they were grooming each other, howling together, and mating. The matchmaking had worked. The wolf biologists were ecstatic, but they worried that with the stress of relocating from Canada, the pair would not produce young the first year. If Number Nine did give birth, the pups would be the first wild wolves born in Yellowstone Park in more than sixty years.

Scientists believe wolves mate for life, or at least as long as both the male and the female live.

National Park Service

Number Ten was the first to leave an acclimation pen, becoming the first wolf to roam free in Yellowstone since 1926.

Biologists used names of geographic locations to identify the packs of reintroduced wolves. Wolves Nine, Ten, and Seven were dubbed the Rose Creek pack. On March 22, 1995, their pen gate was opened. Park historian Paul Schullery wrote in a memo on the day the wolves were released, "Maybe 120 years from now, Yellowstone managers will be able to look back on this project and make some meaningful judgments on the ecological and spiritual consequences of what we've done today. For the moment, all we can do is give ourselves a little credit for having the belated decency to right such a long-standing wrong and pray for puppies."

A radio-tracking plane flies over the Yellowstone wilderness searching for wolves. In the air, scientists can hear the signal from a wolf's collar ten to thirty miles away. Aerial tracking is the only way biologists can keep up with wolves in remote, snow-covered areas of the park.

National Park Service

Once the Rose Creek trio and the park's two other reintroduced packs left their holding pens, biologists began a game of hide-and-seek with the wolves. Because wolves are highly mobile and very secretive by nature, radio collars became the biologists' eyes. Aerial and ground radio tracking of wolves with collars has been in use since the late 1960s. The collars last three to four years and are built not to fall off. Each wolf's radio collar transmits a signal back to a hand-held antenna and receiver. Every radio-collared wolf emits a different signal, much like an individual voice pattern or unique fingerprint. If biologists pick up a signal, they can tell exactly where a particular wolf is.

The number-one goal of the Yellowstone Wolf Project is to remove the gray wolf from the endangered species list. "To do that you have to know how many are out there," says Doug Smith. "That's why it's critical to track and monitor their movements, reproduction, and predation. Our plan is to keep radio collars on all the alpha wolves and on 30 to 50 percent of the young. But we don't want radio collars on every wolf in Yellowstone."

Scientists learned a lot about the wolves after they were freed. The wolves killed prey every two to four days, and they did what the biologists thought they would do. They took the elk easiest to kill: the sick, the weak, the young, and the old. Yellowstone quickly became the best wolf laboratory in North America.

National Park Service

Mike Phillips and Doug Smith inspect a wolf kill. The biologists believed that Number Ten had killed this malnourished bull elk. By sawing a moose's or elk's femur, or leg bone, in half, biologists are able to analyze the bone marrow. Marrow in a healthy animal usually appears white and dense. Marrow that is red or pink and appears gelatinous or jellylike indicates a starving animal, which the researchers believe would be easier to kill.

A Russian proverb says, "The wolf is kept fed by his feet." With long legs, large feet, and an energy-saving lope, wolves can travel more than thirty-five miles a day and can reach speeds up to forty miles per hour.

Biologists also found that the wolves chased and killed coyotes, which compete with them for food and territory. A coyote caught stealing food from a wolf kill was often chased and torn apart. Although coyotes became the losers when wolves returned, grizzly bears benefited. After wolves killed an elk, large bears would chase them away and eat the prey themselves.

Many stories are told about the gray wolf's return to the American West. But the adventures of Number Nine and her Rose Creek pack will live forever in Yellowstone history. Shortly after release from the pen, Nine's daughter, Number Seven, left the pack and went her own way. Most wolves go off on their own when they are about one or two years old. These lone wolves travel around, trying to avoid being killed by other packs, seeking fresh territory, and creating new packs by pairing with wolves of the opposite sex. As for Nine and Ten, they struck out together and settled on the outskirts of a small town called Red Lodge, Montana, just north of the park.

On the morning of April 24, 1995, two men from Red Lodge, Chad McKittrick and Dusty Steinmasel, had just finished freeing their truck from a muddy road in the woods. They were about to leave when they saw something moving along the hillside. McKittrick ran to his truck and grabbed his Ruger 7mm rifle. He aimed and pulled the trigger. In less than a second a bullet struck Number Ten, ripped through the chest cavity, and split the wolf's heart. Only a month after being set free in Yellowstone, Number Ten fell and died.

Wolves sing together, play together, work together, and care for the young in much the way humans do.

Steinmasel had pleaded with his friend not to shoot the animal in case it was somebody's dog. But McKittrick knew it was a wolf and fired his rifle anyway. The two men retrieved the dead body and drove back to McKittrick's house, where they skinned the wolf and cut off its head. McKittrick wanted the wolf's skin and skull. They threw the bloody carcass into a ditch. McKittrick, nervous about the law, asked his friend to destroy the collar. That night, instead of smashing the radio collar, Steinmasel dropped it into a creek near a culvert beside his house.

Two days later wolf biologist Doug Smith flew over the northwest corner of Yellowstone and picked up the signal from Number Ten's collar. The Telonics radio collar was not transmitting at its usual rate of fifty-five

National Park Service wildlife veterinarian Mark Johnson holds one of Number Nine and the slain Number Ten's precious wolf pups. These pups were the first wild wolves born in the Yellowstone ecosystem in over half a century.

National Park Service

beeps per minute. Designed to beep at a faster rate if the collar doesn't move for more than four and a half hours, Number Ten's collar was transmitting over a hundred beeps per minute. Smith and other biologists call this the mortality mode. He knew that either the collar had come off or Number Ten was dead.

The next day, April 27, the still beeping collar of Number Ten led law enforcement special agents to the spot where Steinmasel had thrown it into the creek. Because Steinmasel lived close by, the special agents wasted no time interrogating him. In the first week of May, the agents found Number Ten's carcass in the ditch where McKittrick and Steinmasel had thrown it. On May 13 Steinmasel confessed. Mc-Kittrick was charged a $10,000 fine and sentenced to six months in jail.

While law enforcement officials were tracking the whereabouts of Number Ten, Doug Smith picked up Number Nine's signal from a tracking plane and followed it for more than a week. Number Nine had not strayed from a secluded hillside on the outskirts of Red Lodge. Smith and others believed she might have denned.

On May 3, Joe Fontaine, a wolf biologist, holding a receiver and an antenna tuned to Number Nine's signal, tramped through the thick under-brush on the hillside near Red Lodge. As Number Nine's signal grew stronger, Fontaine picked up another sound coming from the base of a spruce tree. He lifted a branch. Nestled against the trunk was a litter of eight baby wolves, mewing, their eyes still closed.

Biologists feared that with her mate dead, Number Nine would not be able to raise her pups succesfully. In a wolf pack every member contributes to raising the young. At a kill the adults bolt down food and return to the den to regurgitate it to the young, while another adult baby-sits the pups. Unguarded pups are at great risk of becoming prey to a bear or coyote.

On May 18 biologists trapped and tranquilized Number Nine. She was

A wolf pack is a complex family structure with a definite social order. The dominant male and female lead the pack, but every member contributes to raising the young. Strong bonds form among the wolves in a pack.

placed in a dog kennel and taken by helicopter with her pups back to the Rose Creek pen. "One of the most amazing helicopter rides of my life!" Doug Smith said, as he recalled the eight pups scampering loose all over the helicopter.

During the summer and into the early fall of 1995, Number Nine and her pups grew strong and healthy under the watchful eyes of the National Park Service. Three times a week, park biologists hauled road-killed elk to the captive wolves. On October 11 the pack was set free again. Number Nine soon accepted a new mate, a lone wolf from another pack. For the next two years, Nine and her mate led the Rose Creek pack. In the spring of 1998 she had her fourth litter in Yellowstone.

"I've seen Number Nine from the ground and the air so many times, I feel like she's a friend," said Doug Smith. "I'd know her anywhere. We think Number Nine is about eight or nine years old. Wolves rarely live past ten in the wild. She's getting quite gray now, but still in the thick of it. Nine is the matriarch of the new wolf era in Yellowstone. She singlehandedly put wolves back on the map in the park."

From the pioneering research on predator–prey relationships by Paul Errington to Sigurd Olson's study of social behavior and Adolph Murie's fieldwork on Dall sheep

It's a little too early to say how wolves will change Yellowstone. It may take ten or fifteen years to document changes in the elk population. But lots of scavengers in the ecological community — ravens, grizzly bears, magpies, eagles, foxes, wolverines, insects — are benefiting from the leftover wolf kills.

"Of course," says biologist Doug Smith, "all credit is due the wolves. They are supremely adapted to life in the wild. Our plan was good, but once the wolves hit the ground, they did it. Wolves are great at being wolves."

and wolves to Dave Mech's current Arctic wolf research, scientists have increased our understanding of one of nature's ancient beings. And now the dream of Aldo Leopold, David Mech, Renée Askins, Doug Smith, and countless biologists has come true — the gray wolf has come home. Though controversy about wolves is far from over, the success of the Yellowstone project has made restoration of other wolf populations in the United States easier. Programs to restore the eastern timber wolf to New York and the Mexican wolf to Arizona have begun.

Doug Smith and other wolf biologists believe that their work with the wolves is about fixing what humans have destroyed in the past, righting a long-standing wrong. "Wolf reintroduction is not a science. It's an art," Smith points out. "You go on gut feelings, on hunches, learn as you go. We have so much to learn, but the wolves are teaching us. They are teaching us that if we are tolerant, we can live side by side with them. They are teaching us what Thoreau already knew: 'In wildness is the preservation of the world.' By restoring wolves, we restore ourselves."

Current wolf range

Historical wolf range

Alex Tait/Equator Graphics, Inc.

Acknowledgments

First and foremost, I wish to thank Douglas Smith of the Yellowstone Wolf Project. He read the manuscript and offered many helpful comments. I plan to hold him to his promise that the next time I'm in Yellowstone, he'll take me tracking wolves.

Many people assisted in my research for *Once a Wolf,* and I would like to thank Ed Bangs, U.S. Fish and Wildlife Service; Renée Askins, director of the Wolf Fund; Jim Peaco, Yellowstone Park photographer; and Jim Halfpenny and the Yellowstone Institute for the great wolf-watching in Lamar Valley, Yellowstone National Park. Thanks to Jim Brandenburg for his compelling and exquisite color photographs of wolves. I'm especially indebted to Horatio Burns, who welcomed me to his cattle ranch in Big Timber, Montana, and shared with me his love of ranching and another side of the wolf issue. Many thanks as well to my editor, Ann Rider, whose guidance made all the difference.

Sources

Bass, Rick. *The Ninemile Wolves.* New York: Ballantine Books, 1992.

Boos, Kevin. *Alpha—A Story of Wolves and People.* Boise, Idaho: Writers Press, 1997.

Brandenburg, Jim. *Brother Wolf: A Forgotten Promise.* Minocqua, Wis.: North Word Press, 1993.

Busch, Robert. *Wolf Songs.* San Francisco, Calif.: Sierra Club Books, 1997.

Chadwick, Douglas H. "Return of the Gray Wolf." *National Geographic,* vol. 193: no. 5 (May 1998), pp. 72–99.

Defenders of Wildlife. *Wolves of America—Conference Proceedings, 14–16 November, 1996.* Washington, D.C., 1996.

Ferguson, Gary. *The Yellowstone Wolves—The First Year.* Helena, Mont.: Falcon Press, 1996.

Fischer, Hank. *Wolf Wars.* Helena, Mont.: Falcon Press, 1995.

Grooms, Steve. *The Return of the Wolf.* Minocqua, Wis.: North Word Press, 1993.

Halfpenny, James C., and Diann Thompson. *Discovering Yellowstone Wolves—Watcher's Guide.* Gardiner, Mont.: Naturalist's World, 1997.

International Wolf Center. *Wolves Around the World—1997 Update.* Ely, Minn., 1997.

————. *International Wolf—A Quarterly Publication of the International Wolf Center.* Ely, Minn.

Johnson, Sylvia A., and Alice Aamodt. *Wolf Pack—Tracking Wolves in the Wild.* Minneapolis, Minn.: Lerner, 1985.

Link, Mike, and Kate Crowley. *Following the Pack—The World of Wolf Research.* Stillwater, Minn.: Voyageur Press, 1994.

Lopez, Barry Holstun. *Of Wolves and Men.* New York: Scribner's, 1978.

McIntyre, Rick. *A Society of Wolves.* Stillwater, Minn.: Voyageur Press, 1993.

————. *War Against the Wolf.* Stillwater, Minn.: Voyageur Press, 1995.

McNamee, Thomas. *The Return of the Wolf to Yellowstone.* New York: Holt, 1997.

Matthiessen, Peter. *Wildlife in America.* New York: Viking, 1959.

Mech, L. David. *The Way of the Wolf.* Stillwater, Minn.: Voyageur Press, 1991.

————. *The Wolf—The Ecology and Behavior of an Endangered Species.* Minneapolis, Minn.: University of Minnesota Press, 1970.

Murie, Adolph. *The Wolves of Mount McKinley.* Seattle: University of Washington Press, 1944.

Murray, John A. *Out Among the Wolves—Contemporary Writings on the Wolf.* Seattle: Alaska Northwest, 1993.

Patent, Dorothy Hinshaw. *Gray Wolf Red Wolf.* New York: Clarion Books, 1990.

Phillips, Michael K., and Douglas W. Smith. *The Wolves of Yellowstone.* Stillwater, Minn.: Voyageur Press, 1996.

Science Museum of Minnesota. *Wolves and Humans: Coexistence, Competition and Conflict. An Educational Resource for Teachers.* St. Paul, Minn.: 1983.

Steinhart, Peter. *The Company of Wolves.* New York: Knopf, 1995.

Web Sites

Defenders of Wildlife: www.defenders.org

International Wolf Center: www.wolf.org

National Geographic: www.nationalgeographic.com

Ralph Maughan's Wolf Report: www.poky.srv.net/~jjmrm/maughan.html

The Wolf's Den: www.wolfsden.org/wolves

Wolf Haven: www.teleport.com/~wnorton/wolf.shtml

Index